# DICTA TO GRAVY TRAIN.....

## A JOURNEY TO FRUITION

KARAN SHARMA

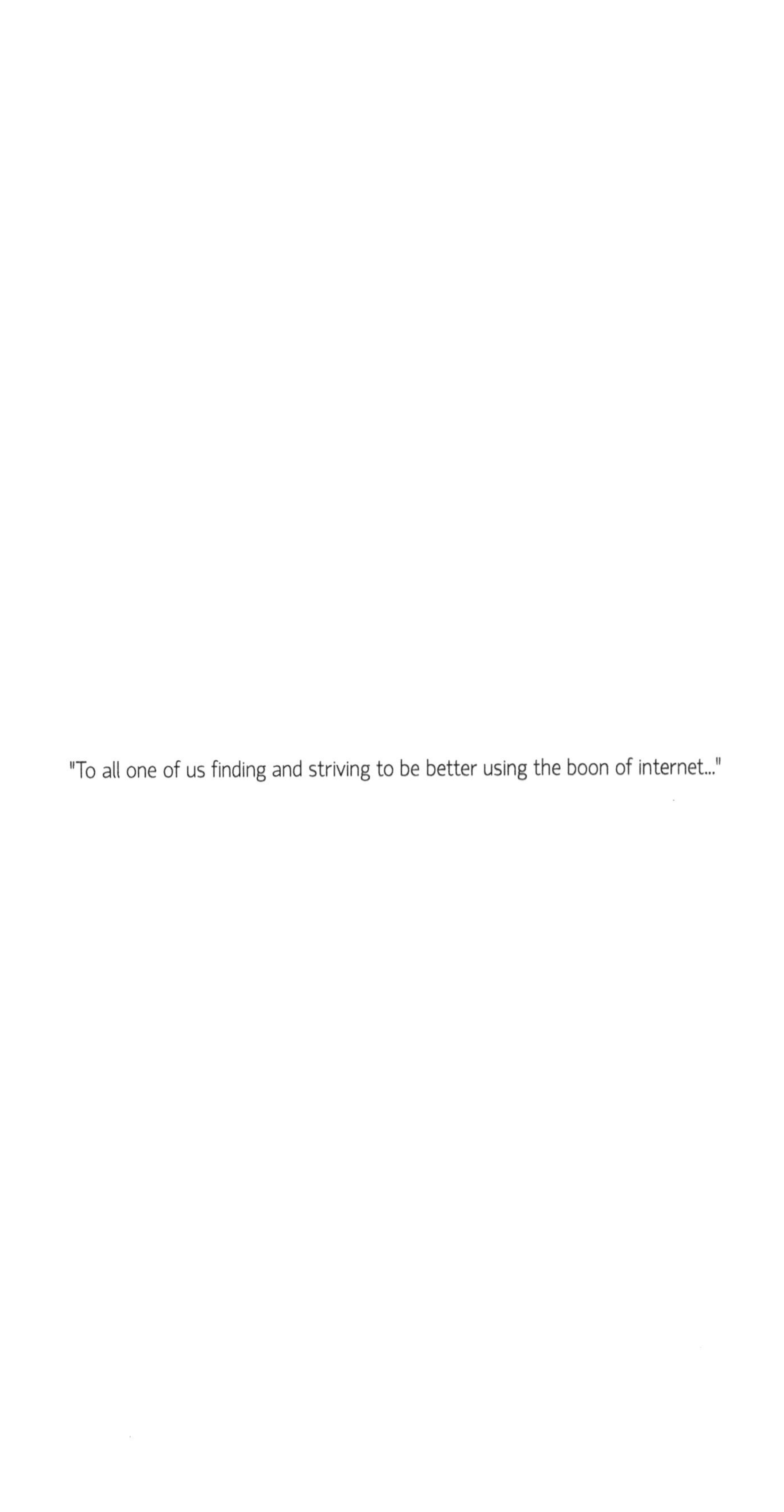

"To all one of us finding and striving to be better using the boon of internet..."

# Contents

# Foreword

From devoting a long span in reading various books to surfing internet for various platforms to showcase one's creativity, I got messed up about what to do and what not. And from that very moment only i got the inspiration to create a series of short titles that prove to cover a massive leap with one's small intiative.....

"SOME WAYS TO DO MORE " is a series of tried and tested methodology by which even a novice child to an old age individual could achieve more than what he or she aspires for...

SO COLLECT AND READ ALL THE TITLES IN THE SERIES.....

# Preface

BEING BORN IN THE AGE OF GLOBALISATION WHERE THE EXCHANGE OF IDEAS AND KNOWLEDGE IS FREE FROM ANY BARRIER AND RESTRICTION , DIFFERENT CULTURES , TRADITIONS OR CROSS-COUNTRY OUTLOOK OVER PERCEIVING THINGS , WE COME ACROSS NUMBER OF DIVERSE THINGS THAT SOMETIMES ANSWER THE QUERIES OR QUESTIONS WE HAVE OR MAKE SOME DIFFICULT TASKS EASY FOR US , IN SEARCH OF THIS INFORMATION OR CLEARING ANY DOUBT OR LOOP HOLE WE USE THE INTERNET SERVICES OR IN OTHER WAYS USE VARIOUS SOFTWARES, SEARCH ENGINES E.T.C , BUT AMID SUCH VAST AND ABUNDANT INFORMATION AVAILABLE WE TEND TO MAKE SOME WRONG DECISIONS OR ENDING UP GET CONFUSED ......

ME BEING GETTING TO SAME TROUBLE THAT WHAT INFORMATION AND SOURCES FROM THIS PUBLICALLY VIABLE AND OPEN FOR ALL NETWORK IS LEGIT OR WHICH WILL YIELD IN ENDING TO RESULTS THAT I WISH TO MAKE ME DRAG TO QUOTE ALL INFORMATION AVAILABLE ON INTERNET CLASSIFIED FOR ALMOST EVERY FIELD THAT WE SOME OR THE OTHER DAY COME ACROSS TO .

BEING CHASED BY SOME MOTIVATION OR SEEING OTHERS HUSTLING TO ACHIEVE THEIR DESIRED GOALS , INDIVIDUALS LIKE YOU AND ME SEARCH OVER THE ESTEEMED SEARCH ENGINES AND BROWSERS OVER SUCCESS , DETEREMINATION , EARNING MORE , CREATING ONE'S UNIQUE IDENTITY THAT WE TEND TO TAKE TIME AND OTHER PRIORITIES FALL SHORT OF TIME.

SO FOR ALL OF YOU WHO ARE IN THE MOTION TO ACHIEVE MASSIVE AND HUGE , THIS BOOK WITH TAKING EVERY DUE CARE I ASSURE THAT WILL FULFILL YOUR MOTIVE OF BUYING IT FOR BEING GOAL ORIENTED .

# Acknowledgements

# CHAPTER ONE

# Becoming the jack of all ...

*How to become smarter or in other words more skilful in doing tasks of different interests*

*Number 1. Judicious use of internet access*

*other than social media screen timing and wasting your wifi on scrutinizing your favourite star about what he or she is wearing ?, where are they roaming around ? ..e.t.c devote your time in researching on "know-how's " of various topics .*

*an important tip which i use to get better information from various sources select and soughted for you is , type "pdf" after everything about which you want to have more information of , such as –*

*suppose i want to have information about bhagvad gita , so would type straight as " bhagvad gita in English pdf " , and google will select the most appropriate results for you and help you gaining more through typing less .*

*making accounts on valuable websites and applications like medium.com , wordpress , qora e.t.c , could help interacting with the knowledgeable expertise beings that share their information based on their extensive research and study , which help in gaining the right information about specific topics in which an individual is keen interested in .*

*number-2 read and recite a new tongue twister each day*

*through reciting a new tongue twister daily , one could get a better command on fluency of speaking , saying new words, help in building communication skills e.t.c ........*

*although you could get a list of tongue twisters on the internet very easily , but being engaged to provide you the crux of internet so that as an individual you can have the best of information available for doing " more from some"!!!!*

*List of important tongue twisters for self enhancement –*

1. *this exercise is for beginners –*

- Keeping customers content creates kingly profits.
- Success seeds success.
- Bigger business isn't better business, but better business brings bigger rewards.
- Wanting won't win; winning ways are active ways
- Seventeen sales slips slithered slowly southwards.
- Don't go deep into debt.
- Ensuring excellence isn't easy.
- Time takes a terrible toll on intentions.
- Feel free to follow that fellow.
- Old bones groan when wind moans.

2. *Exercise for intermediates –*

- She sells seashells down by the seashore.
- If Peter Piper picked a peck of pickled peppers where's the peck of pickled peppers Peter Piper picked?
- A flea and a fly flew up in a flue.
- Rubber baby buggy bumpers.
- Fuzzy Wuzzy was a bear. Fuzzy Wuzzy had no hair. Fuzzy Wuzzy wasn't fuzzy, was he?
- How much wood would a woodchuck chuck if a woodchuck could chuck wood
- Susie's sister sewed socks for soldiers.
- I scream, you scream, we all scream for ice cream!
- I wish to wish the wish you wish to wish, but if you wish the wish the witch wishes, I won't wish the wish you wish to wish.
- Betty bought butter but the butter was bitter, so Betty bought better butter to make the bitter butter better.

3. *Now comes the challenging part , have a look to them –*

- The sixth sick Sheik's sixth sheep's sick.
- An ape hates grape cakes.
- A tutor who tooted the flute tried to tutor two tooters to toot. Said the two to the tutor, "Is it harder to toot or to tutor two tooters to toot?"
- These thousand tricky tongue twisters trip thrillingly off the tongue.
- Six thick thistle sticks. Six thick thistles stick.

- Pad kid poured curd pulled cold.
- Top chopstick shops stock top chopsticks.
- Of all the smells I have ever smelt, I never smelt a smell that smelt like that smell smelt.
- Black bugs blood.
- We supply wristwatches for witchwatchers watching witches Washington wishes watched.

Number 4. *Start engaging yourself in practising new things or activities Engaging yourself in different activities or performing tasks*

*Of different categories and odd from your daily chores helps in looking your daily tasks from a different perspective leading to easy and a better decision making advantage , but the question arises that surrounded and busy in or day to day priorities how could anyone take time and do different activities, so here's the answer to this query of yours*

- *First , make balance through setting targets and have a "undue time " of target set for your goals , undue time means that everyone or everytime a person could not handle tasks or complete in a time bound position so one should have an extra 15-30 minutes planned which works as a matter of ease before doing any task or if any emergency occurs so , one could do his or her work and finish it in allocated time period .*

- *Second , set real goals , unreal and goals for working more than the usual hours would lead fatigue and less productivity than affecting your usual performance is not a good option rather , small goals dividing into daily , weekly and monthly will provide you achieving towards your ambition in real time .*

- *For point third i would lay stress on some of the techniques which the experts say could help every and any individual could actually work on with in real TIME –*

1. *SO FOR THE TECHNIQUE AND STRATEGY NUMBER 1 , I WOULD RECOMMEND FOR ADHERING TO USE OF "**EAT THE FROG** " , SO AS PER THIS TECHNIQUE YOU SHOULD PRIORITIZE WHAT IS MORE IMPORTANT TO YOU , NOW LOOK WHEN I SAY THAT FOR INCREASE IN YOUR INTELLIGENCE LEVEL OR LERANING*

*TO BE MORE SKILLFUL IN LIFE , YOU HAVE TO UNDERSTAND THE IMPORTANCE OF TIME MANAGEMENT ALSO ( ALTHOUGH I WILL BE ADRESSING THE TOPIC OF TIME MANAGEMENT IN THE FOLLOWING CHAPTER OF THIS BOOK, BUT THIS CHAPTER OF BOOK ALSO HAVE THE SAME SIGNIFICANCE BECAUSE IN ORDER TO BE OF MORE VALUE OR LEARNING NEW THINGS , MANAGING TIME SLOTS HOLDS OF UTMOST IMPORTANCE ) , THIS TECHNIQUE CUM PHRASE PROPOUNDED BY MARK TWAIN OR SELF HELP GURU BRIAN TRACY LAY STRESS UPON THE FACT THAT YOU SHOULD OR STOP OR AVOID THE CONCEPT OF DELAYING ACTIVITIES OR DAILY WORKS I.E ;* **STOP Procrastinating** *....... , USE YOURE TIME PERIOD AS ITS BEST AND DO THE WORK HOLDING OF UTMOST IMPORTANCE AS SOON AS POSSIBLE .*

*" EAT THe FROG " TECHNIQUE ALSO ADVOCATE THAT "DO IT BEFORE IT'S TOO LATE !!!" , THAT IS DO YOUR WORK THAT HAS BEEN GIVEN TO YOU OR FULFIL THE DUTIES WHOSE RESPONSIBILITIES ARE MADE TO BE DONE OR PERFORMED BY YOU BEFORE IT'S TO LATE THAT* **"FROG EATS YOU "***!!!!!.*

2. *THE SECOND TECHNIQUE IN THIS DIRECTION TO BE MORE PRODUCTIVE IS the* **"abcde method "** *, according to this methodology you can easily choose the Activities you want to accomplish and complete in tomorrow's day , in other words making daily goals one could access one's productivity and seriousness towards his work .*

*Naming task as* **" a "** *,* **"b"** *,* **"c "** *,* **"d "** *or as* **" e "** *, an individual can easily prioritize it's way of doing various activities without time slots clashing .*

3. *The last but not the least ,* **" ivy lee technique "** *, a 100-year-old strategy for helping people become more productive at work.*

Under the **Ivy Lee method**, at the end of each night you write down your six most important tasks to accomplish the following day in order of importance. The next day, you begin working on the tasks one at a time.

So there's some strategies which i found on the internet which will help each one of us getting desired results of **being more productive or skilful** with increase intelligence.

# CHAPTER TWO

# The early slots

Searching all over search engines , talking to various successful entrepreneur 's , reading various books by greatest authors and analysing various market analyst's advice about "how to make money " , the most frequent searched question over my feed i came across some activities from various websites which i have shortlisted for you , so that each and every one of you taking advantage of your hobby or some skill you have could achieve and earn both money and respect in the society .....

So the ways which i tried and tested that actually enables any high school student or an eighty year old man to earn money are as it follows :-

Number 1. Writing articles – *writing a piece of literature on any favourite or on a topic on which you have great knowledge could be the best option to frame one and upload on various blogpost's or article submitting platforms , with the course of time becoming reader friendly and common among avid readers one could easily earn money or could get monitised for its articles and advices to various magazine companies or publishing platforms .*

*To start with , one must use the platform of " Medium " , a leading platform for submitting short articles and blogs for free . i emphasise on using the platforms which charge no money or are beginners friendly so that individuals could have experience and viewership to the public domain writing without fetching large sums of money and could get actual report and analysis about what people like and demand for .*

*Other platforms which could be used by the beginners for making money with some effort are –*

- *Wordpress.com*
- *Using Wix free content services to make your own website and provide your number of articles , that i have also used and found effective for providing your content at free of cost .*

- *Onmogul.com , a best website i could say on which one could get its article published in real time of quick and immediately with charging not even a penny .*
- *Reddit.com*
- *Uploading it on social media accounts such as facebook , instagram , twitter e.t.c*

*After getting your articles and content on these platforms and assessing the statistic's about the readership among people one could go to make money through accepting their specific policies or fulfilling criteria's .*

*Number 2. Through the medium of podcast –*

*Through using the medium and platform of podcasting , which as per me is the greatest and easiest way to increase your audience and fan base , eventually leading to pay for the exotic content from you .*

*For uploading an episode of podcast by beginners , i used to assess about what to provide , i mean , what people like , what should i talk upon , how to speak , what are the various platforms , how can i upload on various prestigious platforms for free .....e.t.c*

*So for all those who want to make this as their hobby or earn couple of bucks through uploading an episode in their free time this place of book holds sheer importance –*

- *First of all , you have to look over what people love the most , that is , what genre of podcast are loved by the majority of population .*
- *After selecting your choice of topic and framing its script about what to say at without being stammered or fumbled up , speak your content with confidence in your voice recorder of your smart-phone .*
- *Remember that your content should be original , that is , it should not be an excerpt from any podcast material or any others creative content , being original and accepting what one has crafted till time is of utmost importance to a creator.*
- *Now, comes the integral part of your journey to be labelled up as podcaster , as now you have to choose your choice of hosting platform which will provide you a rss feed which will be the address to provide your content to various platforms .*
- *A hosting platform is must to have a rss feed for distributing it various prestigious platform that could be done in a better way through a hosting agency or a company , so being insearch of a hosting agency that provides*

you with best of services , serve your purpose of chosing it and help in distributing your content to millions of people through various platforms here are some of the hosting agency or platforms which as per my choice are better for the beginners to make their reach and lay the foundation stone for earning , have a look these websites for becoming a future successful podcast er -

- spreaker .com , my best of recommendation to it , i have used it personally and use it till now even . its free distribution and upload facilities help make podcasting little easier .one can upload its podcast through making an account to spreaker to google podcast , stitcher.com , itunes store , youtube channel , podchaser , spotify and many more ....

The step of uploading podcast content to the prestigious platform of itunes store and apple podcast one has to have an apple id through which i could get to podcast connect and make your episode's rss feed uploaded to it .

Advice= reviewing your podcast and uploading it may take a time as platforms like spotify and itunes take time to review and publish on their app , so be patient and do not mail them repeatedly for notification regarding your publishment of podcast episode .

- Anchor.com
- Soundcloud

Number 3. Publishing a paperback or an ebook –
through using the skills of your word smartness and passion of writing one can make his or her content framed in as a book . nowdays writing book and uploading it to various platform has become more publically viable , through using self – publishing method that is available at various websites on the internet one can design and manage to write a book and make it to sale in just fractions of seconds . there are various tools and a number of ready templates that could be used by beginners to writing industry to make profits by selling in to any part of the world .

so here are some publishing authorities or companies which charge no money and help in providing the bestest of tools through which one can get enormous support through directly selling via their online stores-

- *Notionpress.com , a best example of providing free support and helping beginners get recognition and platform by publishing their book , the revenue or the royalty policies are favourable for the young writers which is its plus point .*
- *Kindle direct publishing , another best option to get your book as hardcover , paperback or ebook to get uploaded and can be made public viable , charges no fee .*
- *Apple books or ibooks , by writing your book on apple's app named as 'pages' and then uploading to apple books one can publish his or her book with no cost and maximum profit.*
- *Google books*
- *Draft 2 digital , although it is free but it charges 10% of the retail of book as it fee , so it could also be used as a platform for publishing as you have to give the fee that is deduced after your sale and not before the sale to use the medium .*

*OTHER THAN THESE RELATED TO SELLING THE WRITING CONTENT I ALSO FOUND THESE METHODS TO EARN MORE WHICH ARE DIFFERENT FROM TRADITIONAL METHODS BUT ARE QUITE WELL AND COULD BE THINKED OFF-*
*selling your notes*

- *If you are good at writing notes and attended all lectures, you can sell your asserts to less committed students via* <u>NoteSale</u>*. You can create a listing for free, but the site will take a per cent from each of your sales. Typed notes in PDF/Text format sell best, yet it's worth trying with scanned handwritten notes too if you have nice clear writing.*

*SELLING YOUR OLD BOOKS*

- *Instead of just taking them to the thrift shop and receiving peanuts, try using* <u>BooksCounter app</u>*. Scan the book barcode, upload it to the app's system and see which of 20+ different buyback companies offers the highest payout. Once you found the right company, all you have to do is fill in some basic information of how you'd like to get paid, download a free shipping label and pack up all the books to dispatch.*

Number 4. *Through selling photograph's shot by you*

*Through using your photography skills , you can share your content to stock photo agencies like shutterstock , istock and adobe and other similar companies . It really doesn't matter if you are a professional or novice; you still have the opportunity to make some money. Most work on a per download basis where you get paid a percentage every time someone downloads your picture.*

**Number 5. Design Websites**

*Web designers can expect to take home an average of $49,000 per year, according to Payscale. It's tough to get to that point if you're freelancing, but plenty of sites exist to help you to build up your clientele.*

*TopTalpays top dollar for design pros, but be warned: The company boasts that it only hires the top 3% of freelancers.*

*If you're not yet ready for the big leagues, try sharpening your skills by signing up and accepting clients from these freelance websites:*

- *Freelancer: A freelance marketplace where both workers and employers can create listings and specify hourly rates.*
- *Upwork: The largest freelance platform in the world and another marketplace for freelancers in any industry.*
- *Gigster: An on-demand software development website that offers freelance work to designers, developers and product managers.*
- *Guru: A site where freelancers can bid on projects and jobs posted by employers. Employers can also reach out directly to freelancers.*
- *Other than this you can also visit wix.com , weebly.com to make your own website and upload all the goods or services you offer to the people , my website " the karan Sharma bookstore " is also made from wix.com , you can use the free domain and tools available and create a good website that will make your products and services easily available and will provide a sense of legitimacy among customers that " if he is holding a website of own , surely he be providing services worth online business " , captions like these are common if one has something which excludes or makes unique from others .*

**other than these there are also some of the things by which we could make some money .......have a look to these also ....**

*(source - www.savethestudent.org)*

Here are things you can sell to make money today:

- **Childhood toys**–*Your inability to let go of your old favourites could finally pay off. It's always worth raiding your childhood toy collection and having* *a quick look on* eBay*to see what they're selling for. And if you have* any of these toys, *you could be sitting on thousands*

- **Your old clothes** *–If you've got a wardrobe full of clothes you never wear, dig them out try using some of these* websites and apps for selling clothes online. *You can then use the profits to kit yourself in some new stuff instead*
- **Gift cards***–Everyone's favourite didn't-know-what-to-buy-you gift, but does it involve credit for a shop you never shop in? Sell it on, before it expires! Your best bet for this is* eBay.
- ***Coat hangers*** *–Most wardrobes will have way more hangers than is necessary. Hangers that match can fetch up to 50p a pop, so if you don't mind switching over to mix-matched ones so you can cash in on the matching sets, there could be some money involved*
- ***Wine corks*** *–Arts and crafts favourites! If you drink enough of the good stuff to build up a collection, you'll get around 10p for every wine cork and as much as 15p a pop (literally) for champagne corks*
- ***Unused car parking space*** *–Got a private parking space but don't have a car? You'd be surprised how much money you can make from*renting out your car parking space*– especially if you live near a city centre*
- ***Old loo roll***–*We're not even joking. All those cardboard tubes you and your flatmates have been collecting out of sheer laziness can be*sold for 10p a roll*!*

# CHAPTER THREE

# Tips to attain your Brownie Point !!

*The guide for being sensed publically present at almost everywhere or being famous is among all of the things everywhere holds in it's bucket list , and for the same up here are some of the things which helps in building up-*
*Number 1. Through being persistent*

- *Continue to post your photographs on social media in a better way possible such as using various software's to edit your photographs for better resolution and contrast to the background , free apps and websites such as adobe photoshop , Befunky , fotor ,canva and many more are there but as per my personal recommendation i suggest using adobe photoshop and canva which provide user friendly tools that through seeing even a video by a user at youtube could be learned by anyone .*
- *Through recording video on your smartphone with your face being sense clearly , i mean , your face could be seen by people in the video clearly with your name in the caption , so that after you make the follow-up videos or appear in news channels after some days people could relate that , " yes i have saw his or her video !!!" .*

*By imparting some valuable information or making a " top 10 " and uploading it on your youtube channel , social media feeds or making it circulate over whatsapp and other global messaging platforms one could easily increase his or her followship at grassroot level .*
*Number 2. By having interviews or meeting with notable personalities*
*Meanwhile i was searching for all that is neede to become famous or an internet sensation , i devoted a long hour durations on the internet and i founded that through being in-touch with the "big-noise's" one could gather more public*

*support and fame than any other method in today's media time could do .*

*While studying every aspect in detail from various entrepreneurs , personality development mentors and business coaches from live masterclasses , books and by many more methods their are two most prominent method to have your own presence in social media more prominent , these are :-*

- **through appearance in various news channel or getting your article in daily newspaper**

*it has been sensed that through writing articles or multiple visits in news channels people tend to recognise and search about you more on internet leading to your profile tagged as "trending" . but if we look towards the aspect of a bignner with nom experience , or any formal degree for the subject would be more tougher task than becoming famous on the internet so , could refer to the regional channels or tie-up for an interview or appearance in one's friend youtube channel which would provide larger audience helping gaining support .*

*through having frequent web sessions with professionals by requesting a mail invitation could also do well if you are able to persuade them .*

*also to add to this you can find the contact details of the so called "big name " on their website and throw an email requesting for a short web session or a something like that.*

*First of all , be straight to the point don't hesitate in writing to them , but don't write a book upon about yourself and discussing your show e.t.c .....instead write a short and crisp invitation to them about what are you looking for to have with you and why you approached them .*

*Next thing which we will get to talk to them is that "who am i " , you could send your website link , or your previous video for a reference purpose to get them a glimpse about what do you do and what's your theory towards your meet or interaction .*

# About the Author

Karan Sharma , an Author , Podcaster , Article writer and an E-commerce website owner has a spectacular insight which motivates and inspires every men and women want to achieve and do more in life without belonging from an affluent family .

He has been certified with certification of appreciation from prestigious organizations such as UNICEF , WHO, AMNESTY UNIVERSITY , GOOGLE , AMAZON WEB SERICES and a long list of it goes on....

"The Karan Sharma Bookstore " and "The Karan Sharma Show " are examples of few from a whole lot of bunch created by this emerging star with no monetary help or investment .

A 17 year old High School child with energy and spark in eyes to change the world with his creativity and talent , makes various mentors and professionals spellbound and think for out of the box to guarantee yourself of achieving more by doing less !!!

With the selection and submission of Spectacular articles on Medium.com , OnMogul.com Karan Sharma has made his footsteps to zenith inspiring alike individuals to whom opportunity itself is looking for to grabbed upon

.......

# An Intiative for Geeks...

The Karan Sharma Bookstore is a trendsetting online store offering the first rate products and exceptional customer service to individuals all around the globe. They are business made up of innovators and forward-thinkers with the drive and where with all to constantly update and improve the online shopping experience.

This online store has become synonymous with quality and ensure a continuous variety of fantastic products that fit any budget

# Rolling The Carpet

Powered by @Thekaransharmashow, a podcast station providing best of advice and knowledge about Mental Health, entrepreneurship and more. Visit at the - THE KARAN SHARMA SHOW at youtube or listen the podcast titles listen before hand at Itunes Store, Spotify, Google Podcast, Spreaker.com, Stitcher.com and many more...